THE PIG AND I

A TRUE STORY

By

JEANNETTE HALEY

Hidden Manna Publications

THE PIG AND I

Hidden Manna Publications
PO Box 3572
Oldtown, ID 83822

Facebook:
https://www.facebook.com/HiddenMannaPublications/

DEDICATION

I want to dedicate
this book to my friend
Pam Wester,
who understands both
the pig and me, and
who loves me any way.

CONTENTS

1

I SAID, "I DO"

Everyone in the church was staring straight at my wedding bouquet—I just knew it. The thing was violently shaking and try as I might, there was no stopping it.

I couldn't understand why I was so terrified. Just because my "to-be-in-six minutes" husband had four children ages ten, twelve, fourteen, and sixteen, sprawled unhappily on the front pew behind us, didn't mean I should be nervous. The oldest girl was especially sullen, but I was sure she'd soon see it my way and become a transformed beam of sunshine. After all, she was getting a stepmother with plenty of experience with children.

Even though I was an only child, I had babysat twice in my younger years and had even taught a small Sunday school class. On top of that, I was a thirty-year-old-idealist. Three girls and a boy should be a snap, right?

The ceremony ended with a flourish and I was officially Mrs. Liebenthal. Since it was too late to reconsider this whole deal, I decided to make the most of the reception. Mind you, I have been blessed with one of those faces that never fail to tell it all, and the photographs of this grand occasion bear proof of that.

After a too-brief honeymoon to Canada, we hurriedly moved into the old remodeled farmhouse situated on three acres. It came complete with a rather elaborate chicken house built on cement block "stilts". There was a large pond in the field behind the house as well as a harmless little bubbling creek. In the front yard was a goldfish pond. A wood fence that had been painted white completed this tranquil scene. In the back of my mind I pictured four pairs of hands repainting that fence. Yeah, right.

I remember how excited I was the first time I saw our jumbo mailbox across the road. Soon after, however, the young intelligentsia of the night smashed it rather badly. Since my new husband, Kevin, wasn't into fixing anything in particular, but some things more or less in general, the mailbox remained pathetically perched on top of the post in its crumpled state.

The house itself had a full basement, complete with fireplace, tack room, shelves for canned goods, laundry room, small bedroom with a half bath. That's where his son, Craig, decided to make his lair.

The main floor was delightful to me and I began to care for it and guard it like an obsessed Banty rooster. For some mysterious reason, known only to God and the previous inhabitants, the living room was carpeted in pure white. There was no way I was going to let anyone walk on that sacred rug with dirty shoes. (Later, much to my amazement, I discovered white carpet in many of the farm homes in that area and we're talking about a very wet, muddy part of the country.)

There was a magnificent deck off the hallowed living room, shaded by an enormous maple tree. The kitchen was large and also had white floors, which I scrubbed nearly every night. Off of the kitchen was a small dining room with just enough space for the family to crowd around the long, maple table. What I really loved was the homey little black earth stove cockily situated on red bricks.

A small guest bedroom was located off the kitchen area next to an ascending staircase that let to the forbidden bedrooms of the two younger girls, Teresa and Connie. As for the sixteen-year-old, Samantha, she moved out the second night after we moved into the house and went across the road to stay with her grandmother. I have to admit I didn't waste any tissue on that one.

The master bedroom and two bathrooms completed my dream home. My goal was always, day or night, to be prepared should a roving photographer from Better Homes and Gardens Magazine suddenly appear on the scene.

It didn't take a genius to figure out that this whole scenario, farmhouse, acreage, animals, and kids was going to be a lot more than I could handle. But, at this point in my life, I thought I was the female version of Atlas. *No problem,* I told myself, *it wouldn't be long until I'm on top of it. After all, I have always wanted to leave the city life and live in the country. I've seen plenty of Westerns and know all about the Wild West. Nuthin' to it, just watch!*

And plenty of people did just that!

2

WHAT IS NORMAL?

If I live to be a hundred, I'll never forget the day the neighbors, who lived upstream, came to pay a call. Kevin had gone to pick the kids up from school and I was alone at the time.

As usual, I was busy "de-germing" the kitchen when I heard a tap on the kitchen door. Startled, I looked out through the spotless diamond-shaped windowpanes and saw two beaming faces. Returning their friendly smiles I quickly opened the door.

"Hi!" exclaimed the woman whom I could tell was in her early thirties. "We're your neighbors, Peggy and Ted Black, and we've come to introduce ourselves and welcome you."

I introduced myself and invited them in. They settled themselves around the dining room table while I quickly brewed a pot of tea. Once settled, they looked at me approvingly as I tried to sound somewhat civilized and intelligent. I had a captive audience since Kevin and the kids were gone. Peace and order reigned while I explained about our recent marriage and relocation to the country.

"We built our own house down on the creek," Peggy said. "You'll have to come up and see us."

I stared with envy at her flawless complexion and rosy cheeks. To get my face to look half that good I had to plaster on a ton of Cover Girl followed by a good dose of rouge.

Peggy suddenly looked smug, and added with pride, "We raise pigs."

Ted folded his large, muscular arms and leaned back in the chair. His lips formed a twisted smile and his blue eyes narrowed. "That's what my wife loves to do," he said matter-of-factly. He ran a large hand over his blond crew cut. "We have one son, Corey. He's in 4-H and raises a hog each year to show at the county fair."

"Oh," I stammered. "That's very nice."

"Bring your husband up soon and we'll show you our pigs," Peggy grinned, showing an even row of perfect white teeth. It was obvious pigs were her life.

Since the closest I had ever been to a pig was flipping bacon in a frying pan, I tried to change the subject. Somehow I didn't think it was a good time to discuss the Jewish tradition that pigs weren't kosher.

"I just love that sweet little creek out back," I said enthusiastically.

"Ha!" Ted laughed. "Honey, did you hear that? 'Sweet, little creek!' Just wait until we have one of them big storms. Then you'll find out!"

Peggy laid her hand on Ted's arm. "Oh, don't listen to him. We've lived there for years and we've never been flooded out yet."

A picture of the chicken house perched four feet off the ground flashed through my mind. "You mean that little stream can actually overflow?" I asked incredulously.

"There's nothing to worry about," Ted recanted, "As long as your husband keeps the culvert cleaned out. But if anything should wash downstream and get caught in there, then your whole pasture and yard could be under water."

I pictured the stream in my mind as it flowed down the entire length of the pasture and disappeared through the culvert under the road, reappearing in the neighbor's pasture. (We lived on a corner; hence, we had two roads flanking the property.)

"Okay," I reassured them, "I'll be sure to tell Kevin about that."

We discussed a few other topics of local interest and then Peggy said, "You know, we've lived here a long time and there have been a lot of people come and go out of this house." She glanced at her husband who had a smug grin on his face. She continued, "They have all been strange, and now since we've met you, we can't tell you how happy we are to finally have normal neighbors."

"That's for sure," Ted agreed as they rose to leave. "It's sure a relief to know a normal family."

After they left, I determined to prove just how "normal" we could be. But, what is normal?

3

THE ZOO

What would this world be like without animals? Uninteresting and blah, no doubt, and especially to ranchers and hunters. What would it be like without birds and fish? Quiet and boring, especially to birdwatchers and fishermen. What would our lives be like without adoring, lovable pets? Unimaginable! What would life be like without snakes? Wonderful!

On the practical side, for centuries animals have provided food, clothing, shelter, and a host of other things. And, where would Walt Disney be today without those sweet and alluring creatures that form the basis for countless cartoon characters and movies?

As for our new abode, it quickly took on a character of its own as we moved two horses, one dog, and a score of chickens into their respective places.

Now, mind you, I've always, all my life, wanted my very own horse. But, hubby made it quite clear that the horses belonged to his kids. I could pet them, groom them, and ride them, but they weren't mine and never would be. It seemed those horses had enough horse sense to understand this unchangeable rule. It worked like this; they never took me seriously. Try as I might, it was next to impossible to get them to go more than the distance of three city blocks from our pasture.

As for the chickens, much to my amazement, there were different kinds! Coming from the city, I figured a chicken was a chicken. Whatever they were I can't rightly recall, except the big ones were Rhode Island Reds. But the real shocker was when I was told roosters don't lay eggs. I had a lot to learn.

The old tales about "getting up with the chickens" was a joke. Except for those loud-mouthed roosters, the girls in the hen house didn't get with it until about 3:00 in the afternoon. At least that's when a person could gather fresh eggs.

Now, you'll notice I said "a person". That doesn't necessarily include yours truly. Like the horses, there seemed to be a total lack of respect for Mrs. Liebenthal in the hen house. I was so scared of being "hen pecked" while trying to snatch eggs from under those plump, feathered fiends that I resorted to using a flat board to prop up those sitting chickens while hastily retrieving the eggs. They about pecked that board to pieces, but at least I escaped the nasty little blows from those hard beaks.

Now, about the dog, Bandit. He came with the kids and was a mess. Underneath the black, matted unkempt fur was an average sized poodle. While I love dogs, this one was definitely not my type, and he knew it. However we had an agreement. He stayed out of my space, and I stayed out of his.

Then one day the inevitable happened. I ran into a real live garter snake. Shrieking my lungs out, I made it to the safety of the house where I sat shaking and crying. I hate snakes! I don't care what kind they are, what color they are, or what their names are. It matters not if they are expertly photographed and displayed on the pages of the finest of magazines. My reaction is always the same; that is, up in the air it goes.

By this time I had brilliantly figured out that nothing respected me, including those kids. But nonetheless, I had threatened them with death if they ever chased me with a

16

snake. They knew I meant it. This time, the point had hit its mark.

Of course, all my screaming running, door slamming and shaking caused everybody to snap to attention. Approaching me with caution, Connie said, "We know Bandit can hunt and kill snakes for you." I thought about that statement for a moment. Yes, I recalled seeing that black mop hunting around the borders of our place every morning. Perhaps there was a slim chance he could team up with me. For sure something had to happen or I'd be a prisoner in that house until the day I died. There was no way anybody was going to get me outside again, ever, as long as snakes slithered through the place.

The deal was struck, the terms laid out. I told those kids if they taught Bandit how to hunt, catch, and kill snakes, he could have whatever he wanted. It mattered not if all we had for the family was hamburger, he'd get steak, roast, chicken. Nothing would be too good for a fine dog like that!

In the days that followed every morning my favorite sight was Bandit, eagerly scouting the yard, flower beds and fence line for the prey. I have to admit he did a good job. After the kill was made, he promptly retreated to the porch where he sat proudly grinning from ear to ear, waiting for the juicy reward. I never disappointed him. He was more popular with me than Saint Patrick was with Ireland, and he did just as good a job!

One day the girls announced, as they headed out the door for school, "O, by the way, the vet is coming today to worm the horses and you'll have to help to hold them." Great news, a new lesson in the nitty-gritty of horse care. Just want I needed to hear.

Not only did the vet show up on time, but, true to their word, he enlisted my help. I had hoped this was one of those occasions when the girls were just shooting off their mouths. But no such luck, I was it.

Just remembering the whole ordeal makes me sweat. I was 5' 3 ¼" tall and weighed 105 pounds. It goes without saying that the horses were considerably bigger. The vet seemed oblivious to my nervous chatter and chartreuse face. He just simply wanted to get the job done, get his money, and get on his way.

"Here, hold this—tight!" he instructed as he handed me a handle which was in some sort of cruel way attached to the horse's nostrils. Then he proceeded to shove a tube down the poor beast's throat. All I remember is being tossed around like a leaf in the wind as the horse decided this wasn't his idea of a good time.

I must've gone into shock because I can't quite recall the entire incident, but somehow those two horses survived, the vet survived, and I survived.

I tried to calm my shattered nerves by busying myself in the kitchen. At this point it definitely would not be a good idea for me to sit and replay the entire rodeo over again in my mind.

Suddenly the girls came bursting through the door. Out of the corner of my eye, I saw them exchange a knowing smirk. A little light clicked on in my head that lit up the silent words, *you were set up.*

"Hi!" exclaimed an over-enthusiastic Connie. Without waiting for a reply, she blurted, "Did the vet come out today?"

"Yeah," chimed in Teresa. "How'd it go?"

I looked into her bright, blue eyes. They were full of mischief and I could see she was struggling to keep her China doll face somber. Her straight, naturally blood hair shimmered in the afternoon light.

Connie cocked her head and fastened her hazel eyes on my face. Even her short, light brown hair seemed to be defiant.

I smiled and turned back to the potatoes I had been peeling. "Fine."

"What?" exclaimed Connie. "I mean, did you hold the horses for him?"

"Sure," I said happily, "Nuthing' to it."

"Oh," replied Connie. Her tone registered both confusion and disappointment.

Teresa grabbed her sister by the sleeve, "Come on, Connie. Let's change and go riding."

I listened at the foot of the stairs to their muffled exclamations of surprise and promised myself that the next time those horses needed to be wormed, I'd be the one to make the appointment with the vet—on a day when everybody would be home—except me!

4

THE COUNTRY CHAPEL

One of the first things I did when we initially moved into the country was to contact the pastor of the little community church. I had always attended Sunday school and church and decided church attendance was definitely a requirement of the Liebenthal family. Kevin agreed with me on this point and usually went with us even though he worked nights.

Getting everybody up and out was quite a challenge, especially with the girls. They were definitely creatures of the night, and when Sunday morning rolled around there were plenty of moans and groans.

The white, wood church was old and quaint. I instantly loved the steeple, complete with a real bell that melodiously rang every Sunday morning. The lovely setting of green grass and evergreens remind me of the kind of scene one sees on calendars, post cards, and Christmas cards.

The interior of the small church contained old wooden pews, wooden floors, and a carved wooden pulpit. There was an antique clock on the wall, (which was later stolen by Teresa's boyfriend) there was a wood stove in the fellowship room that adjoined the sanctuary.

The Liebenthal family took up an entire pew and I remember how much I wanted to appear "normal." You know, "Mr. And Mrs. Christian and their lovely children." After all, one of the reasons I married Kevin was to force myself to be "normal". I was tired of living the single life, working in a boring government job in the big city, while, to my way of thinking, everybody knew "normal" meant being married and having a family.

Therefore, I decided it was time for me to learn how to sew so I could make Sunday-go-to-meeting clothes for myself and the girls. The country atmosphere brought renewed inspiration to my vivid imagination. Images of slim-waisted ladies sporting parasols, strolling along wooden sidewalks in long dresses propelled me to tackle the stacks of yardage I had purchased when shopping in the small town ten miles away. I pictured myself in a ruffled blouse and ankle length skirt with my long, red hair pinned into a proper and "religious" bun. Yes, it was going to be wonderful being "normal".

A few hours into the project, however, left me confused, frustrated, and in tears. I obviously hadn't inherited my mother's talent for sewing! The pattern didn't make any sense and I was sure it wasn't in English; at least it wasn't printed in any language I understood. There was nothing left to do but call my mother, long distance, and suck up all the knowledge I could.

The phone call was made, Mom was home, and her advice was to the point. It went like this, "Throw out the pattern and just make the thing." There was no arguing with Mom once she had given her opinion. "Okay," I stammered. "Thanks."

Needless to say, it was a battle, but I won. Exhausted and numb, I fell into bed, hoping beyond hope I didn't forget the difference between inner facing and inter facing.

Sunday morning finally came and I slipped into my new, bright yellowish green, polyester skirt and white blouse. I managed to prevail over my straight, unmanageable hair, pulling it into a bun. I was ready.

Settled into the small, hard pew I remember what a wonderful feeling it was, sitting straight and tall with my not-too-happy brood. I figured I nearly fit into the old-fashioned, all-American, traditional church image. All that was missing was a horse and buggy.

Now that sewing had become one of my causes, I attacked it with a vengeance. The girls soon became interested in my obsession, and seizing the moment decided I could possibly be used for their benefit.

"Can you please make me this skirt for Sunday?" Connie sweetly asked, pointing out a pattern that piqued her interest.

I wanted to be a good mom, a "normal", self-sacrificing kind of mom, so in spite of the fact that it was late Saturday afternoon, I agreed. Perhaps my willingness to comply with her request and the great sacrifice it would take on my part might just win her approval. At least it was worth it to me to give it a good try.

Everything seemed to be against efficient progress, however, and the hours slipped past. I was exhausted, but knew that Connie expected me to have her project ready for church. At long last, in the wee hours of the morning, I finished putting in the hem, pressed it, and hung it up. Then I hit the sack.

Before I knew it, hubby had come home from work and it was time to get up and get ready for church. I mechanically went through the motions of getting ready, putting on my best all-American pioneer woman get up. Kevin yelled for the girls and they thundered down the stairs. I looked expectantly at Connie to see how she liked her new skirt, but she wasn't wearing it.

"Why aren't you wearing the skirt I made for you last night?" I blurted.

"I don't like it so I change my mind," she replied nonchalantly.

"Wha-a-a-a-t?" I screamed in anger, "I stayed up all night to get that thing made because you just had to have it for today!" I was close to tears.

"Get upstairs and put on that skirt!" Kevin yelled.

Connie responded loudly, screaming her protest all the way up the stairs. It was a terrific way to start the day.

All the way to church Kevin admonished Connie about her conduct, attitude, and ingratitude but it didn't put a dent in her pout. Theresa and Craig nervously tried to keep straight faces, but it was obvious they both wanted to break out into hysterical laughter. I never did figure out if they were laughing at Connie or me, or both!

5

THE PIG ARRIVES

"We need a pig," Kevin stated one morning behind the paper he was reading.

"Whatever for?! I asked as my mind made a mental list of all the animals, chores, and unending projects at hand.

"Ham, bacon, pork roast," he replied matter-of-factly.

"You mean," I replied incredulously, "we'd kill it?" I just wasn't prepared to raise some poor animal and then do it in.

"Of course, kill it," Kevin said with amusement. Out of the corner of my eye I saw the kids look at each other.

"Pigs kill snakes," Craig chimed in hopefully. "You won't have any snakes in the yard if we get a pig."

"Really?" I was interested. Even though Bandit was doing an excellent job of ridding the property of snakes, they had a way of showing up at the most inopportune moments, like when my mother and her husband drove up to visit one afternoon. I looked out the kitchen window just in time to see my mother dash past the rockery, screaming at the top of her lungs. Crashing through the door, she gasped out in horror, "There's a snake in the flowers out there." That was the first and the last visit we ever had from her.

"Where would he live?" I asked. Kevin lowered the paper and his blue eyes looked at me in amazement.

"Out in the pigpen by the chicken house."

"Oh, "I said, then added, "perhaps the Blacks would have a pig we could buy."

"Yeah maybe," Kevin said, "but I want to take a run out to this place I found in the paper and check out their wieners.

Later that afternoon with all three kids crammed into the small Japanese-manufactured station wagon we made our way through the woods to a barely visible gravel driveway that wound its way up a steep hill. Kevin pulled to a stop in a cloud of dust. I quickly glanced around the run-down farm. Rusting equipment and leaning outbuildings were overgrown with blackberry bushes. The old wood farmhouse badly needed repair and paint.

The screen door squeaked in protest as a middle-aged woman stepped through the doorway and sauntered out to the car. A breeze tugged at her salt and pepper hair. Squinting at us in the unusually bright sunshine, she offered a friendly "Howdy" with a toothless grin. "Come up to see the weenies?"

Kevin nodded, and we all exited the car. I couldn't but help notice that she looked very pregnant, but I knew that wasn't probably possible judging by her age. She was wearing a stained apron over a faded, cotton dress. The hem was uneven and she wore anklets and homely brown shoes. It was obvious that this woman never gave a thought to waxing moustaches or shaving legs.

We found ourselves following her through a maze of weeds, fences, and piles of stuff I had no name for, past a vegetable garden and out to a small pen. The stench was horrible, and I knew that our pig wouldn't possibly smell as bad.

Several black pigs with a white, belt-like band snorted their welcome.

"Hampshires," the woman who had introduced herself as Gretchen said proudly.

"Hampshires?" I repeated. How come they aren't pink?

The kids snickered and Kevin and Gretchen exchanged amused looks. "Honey," Kevin corrected methodically, "all pigs aren't pink. It depends on the breed."

"Oh," I said quietly. When was I ever going to learn to keep my mouth shut? Not only were there different kinds of chickens, but apparently there were different kinds of pigs too. It was all very confusing.

I lapsed into deep contemplation of how Noah ever got so many different kinds of animals on the ark while Kevin and the kids selected the one they thought would suit them best. Soon we were on our way with our newest farm member grunting his disapproval in the back of the car.

"Phew!" I exclaimed. "Open the windows, will you? We need to give that thing a bath."

"Bath?" Kevin laughed. "he's not going to live in the house, you know."

"Well, we at least need a pickup truck for all this farm stuff you do."

His brow furrowed and I knew I had brought up the wrong subject at the wrong time. "We do not need a truck. I can get anything in this station wagon and then some. This car is economical."

Fortunately, Gretchen's place was not too far from ours and the unhappy pig was soon in his new home. I stomped into the house and started dinner while the kids and Kevin did whatever they had to do to secure that pig in the pigpen. After all, I concluded, my place was in the house, not out there in the mud.

That evening Kevin decided to give me a lesson on how to sort edible garbage. Gretchen had informed us that a truckload of discarded produce from some grocery outlet in the city came weekly to her place. She said we were welcome to come out and go through it for ourselves. Kevin was ecstatic. Of course, since Kevin worked nights and slept during the day, the person who would be driving to her place would be me.

"Okay," he directed, as he brought me several large, plastic containers with lids.

"I want you to put potato peelings, apple cores, and cooked leftovers in here for the pig." He pointed to a large container. "Then I want you to sort out what the chickens like, you know, leftover lettuce, greens, and that sort of thing, but first, when you get the stuff home from Gretchen's, be sure to save out what is still good enough for us to eat."

I sighed and rolled my eyes up to the ceiling. Now my life would consist of sorting edible from inedible garbage. No more leisurely strolls through the produce section of the grocery store.

Kevin ignored my emotional attitude and went on, "You know that the horses also get some carrots and apples and then there's the dog that gets meat scraps and bones."

"Fine," I said. I was tired and this new job as garbage executive could be tricky. I'd have to think it all through another time.

"Tomorrow we'll start rototilling the garden," Kevin went on smugly, "and just think! Soon there'll be plenty of stuff for the pig and the chickens so it'll cut down on the cost of feeding them."

"Who's going to take care of that garden?" I asked suspiciously.

"The kids will help you."

6

THE GARDEN, THE GOAT, AND THE GOOSE

Things progressed at a rapid pace and soon we had a garden with twenty-two rows of all kinds of interesting things. Thanks to my Grandma, I had learned a little bit about gardening. We planted carrots, beets, radishes, kohlrabi, string beans, onions, potatoes, lettuce, Swiss chard, Jerusalem artichokes, peas, corn, and squash.

The garden consumed a great deal of my time. Stubborn persistent weeds pushed to the surface so rapidly I could've sworn you could hear them grow. Slugs were another constant problem, but I fought them with the resolve of David fighting Goliath. Armed with slug bait, salt, and shovel, I marched around that patch of land determined to eradicate every pest.

One day I glanced out the kitchen window just in time to see the young gelding gleefully rolling around on his back in the garden! Somehow he had escaped from the fenced pasture. Screaming for help I tore out the door, ran down the steps and raced across the yard. The horse jumped to his feet, shook himself off, and sauntered out into the grass. The girls had caught up with me by that time and quickly grabbed his halter, telling him how naughty he was. They cast furtive glances my way to see if I was going to murder their big pet with my trowel.

Needless to say, I was furious. The small plants, which had just recently sprouted, were flattened to the ground. But, there wasn't anything that could be done except keep tilling the ground and praying for them. Miraculously, much to my amazement, those tough vegetables made a wonderful comeback.

One day while working in the garden, I hit the end of my rope what with all the housework, garbage sorting, and gardening. Since the kids were home, lazily lounging in bed, I decided to make good on Kevin's promise. Glancing at the house, I saw Craig standing against the railing on the deck, watching me.

"Hey, Craig," I yelled. "Get dressed and come out here and give me a hand with this garden."

He yelled back and I swear I heard, "I don't give a damn."

I threw down my hoe and made a beeline to the house while he continued to stand on the deck, marking my progress. He had a quizzical look on his face.

"Don't you ever let me hear you cuss again!" I screamed. "Never! Do you hear me!"

"What?" he said in genuine surprise. "I didn't swear. What I said was "I don't think I can.""

"Are you sure?" I looked at his innocent face.

"Honest, I didn't swear. What did you think I said?"

"Never mind. Why can't you help today?"

"Because I have a practice match this afternoon at the high school." Then he added, "Can you drive me into town?"

Nothing but nothing irritates me as much as interrupted plans, but what is one to do? Nodding my agreement, I plodded back to the garden for one last round with the insistent weeds.

****

30

One afternoon Kevin announced, "We need a goat."

"What for?" I asked.

"Well, we need a goat to eat all those blackberry bushes all around this place."

"Blackberry bushes?" I gasped. "Wouldn't that be hard on his mouth?"

"They don't eat the prickly part, they eat the leaves," Kevin patiently explained.

"What good does that do?" I replied.

"It gets rid of all that foliage so it's easier to cut off the vines."

"Where are we going to get a goat?" I asked carefully avoiding the subject of different kinds of goats. I didn't have a clue about that. To me goats were goats.

"Oh, I met somebody who has a neutered goat that I think we could have."

I countered, "Don't you think we have enough animals to take care of? After all, we really don't have very much land here and a goat would just be one more thing to worry about."

Craig had been sitting nearby, listening in silence. He decided to come in with his favorite punch line. "If we had a goat, then for sure there wouldn't be any snakes around here. Snakes hate goats. And, besides, a neutered goat doesn't smell as bad as one that isn't fixed"

I contemplated this new bit of information. For one thing, I hadn't thought about goats stinking. I'd never been around a goat so how would I know about that? However, the possibility that this would be a further snake deterrent sold me. "Okay, let's do it."

Little did I know that the goat would provide enough excitement to last for a long, long time.

31

About the same time, Kevin decided we needed some geese.

"What do we need geese for?" I asked. Somewhere in the back of mind a wee bit of knowledge surfaced which produced an image of someone getting severely pinched in the behind by a goose.

"They'd be nice to have in the pond," Kevin explained. "And they are better than watch dogs."

"We already have a watch dog and he is good at his job," I argued.

"But geese are fun to have and they lay eggs."

"Ah," I countered, "we have chickens for that."

"But," Kevin's patience was wearing thin. "The chickens don't lay all the time, and I plan to start selling fresh eggs. Plus, goose eggs are so big, that one is worth three chicken eggs."

As usual, I lost and the goat and the geese won. Soon we had one belligerent goat tied to the outer fringes of the property and noisy, bossy geese proudly floating around in the pond.

It was no problem finding customers for the eggs. The folks with the milk cows down the road agreed to trade milk for fresh eggs. This launched World War III with the kids.

"What? Drink *that* milk?" Connie whined in protest.

"Yeah," Theresa chimed in. "We're used to store bought milk. We don't want it."

"Nevertheless, "Kevin said firmly, "You're going to drink it and you'll get used to it, and that's that."

"Oh Dad, please," moaned Connie, "Do we have to?"

"Yep. It's either fresh milk or nothing."

My job was to drive down to the farm on certain days of the week and get the milk that came in big gallon jars. There was at least four or five inches of cream on the top, and I soon learned how to turn it into butter.

One day the farmer's wife called. "Hi," she said cheerfully, "I need to let you know you're either keeping your chicken house too hot or I've got the wrong eggs."

"What happened?" I gasped.

"Well," she said, "when I went to make breakfast today and I tried to crack those eggs, I discovered they're all hard boiled."

Kevin had grabbed the wrong box out of the refrigerator and given them to her. After that we carefully distinguished any hard cooked eggs from the fresh ones.

The geese did lay wonderful eggs and I enjoyed using them for baking cakes, breads, and such *if* they were fresh. Since the geese were left to roam around in the pasture they cleverly hid their eggs in different places. The kids would find them and bring them into the house. One of my worst memories is that of cracking open a large goose egg that contained a partially formed baby goose. The sight and the stench was nearly more than I could bear.

Every morning about 5:00 a.m. when Kevin pulled into the driveway, those geese (by now there were four of them), would squawk and honk so loud I am sure it woke the entire countryside. He was right, they were excellent "watch dogs", but how I hated to be awakened in the early morning hours by those shrill sounds.

One afternoon I heard the geese shrieking and flapping in a panic. Racing to the window, I spotted our neighbor's huge Afghan hound pursing the terrorized birds. I raced outside, picking up rocks as I went. The dog got the message and loped across the pasture, crawled under the fence and trotted across the road into his yard. He belonged to our neighbor, Rachel, who attended our church.

Now I liked Rachel a lot, so I called her and asked if she could keep her dog home, that he liked to come over and chase geese. She giggled and twittered, and mumbled something about that silly dog. I knew the point had been missed.

About that time, another neighbor on the other side of the road, heard about my plight with Rachel's dog from his wife. He showed up at my door one afternoon with an air rifle.

I'd never heard of an air rifle, much less seen one. He quickly explained how it worked and assured me that it wouldn't kill the dog, but that it would let him know he wasn't to trespass and chase geese.

I remember lying on the floor to get enough leverage to pump the thing up, and then I put it under the bed, just in case the shag carpet on four legs showed up again.

I didn't have long to wait. Within a couple of days, Rachel's dog was back in our pasture, racing around the pond, harassing our poor geese.

I ran to the bedroom, grabbed the rifle, dashed to the deck and took aim. It was quit a sight, geese flapping and squawking and that big galoot of a dog in hot pursuit. I had never fired any kind of a weapon and the only thing I had been good at, well sort of, was bowling. But determination overcame inexperience and at the right moment I squeezed the trigger.

That poor critter took a direct hit. He let out a loud yelp and frantically dashed towards home. I resisted my automatic feelings of guilt, telling myself I had just saved those poor geese form certain death, and that Rachel's dog was going to live.

He did, indeed, live and came back in a few days to give it another whirl. The trusty air gun was in its usual place. Grabbing it up I headed out to the deck. This time the kids were in tow. Pow! Got him again. The kids were cheering, the dog was yelping and heading for home and the geese were cackling their gratitude. For some time to come my new name was "Annie Oakley."

One day Rachel approached me in church. I felt some trepidation, but managed to keep a rather straight face.

"Say," she said with a grin. "I just can't figure out what has happened to my dog."

"Oh?" I replied.

"Yeah, he never seems to want to run off to your place anymore. In fact, he stays home all the time. I wonder whatever changed his mind."

Meanwhile, the milk trips were going well, and the kids had adapted to the taste of fresh, raw milk. However, you just haven't lived until you've had a whole gallon of the creamy white stuff tip over and spill all over the carpet behind the driver's seat of your car! I sopped it up, mopped it up, and cleaned it up with everything I could throw at it. I don't know how many cans of Lysol spray I went through before the distinct smell of sour milk dwindled to a less distinct odor. I learned that once a gallon of raw milk baptizes the carpet in your car, you will never know what it's like to drive a car that reminds you of a Holstein.

****

As time went on, that goat proved to be more than a handful. Kevin insisted on tethering him outside of our fence with just enough rope to get to the edge of the roadway. We could periodically hear the squeal of brakes and the honking of horns as people thought the goat was ready to jump in front of their vehicles. Several times folks politely stopped to tell us our goat was loose.

But the clincher came in the middle of one dark night. Kevin and I were awakened to the sound of loud raps on the kitchen door. Now, mind you, the top half of the ornate door was made of triangle panes of glass. It was one of the reasons I wanted that house in the first place. The whole front of the place was charming and homey.

Kevin tumbled from bed and hurried to the door. He didn't turn on any lights so he could see who was there through the glass. I stayed in bed and listened. Soon I heard muffled conversation, scuffling and thumping and then Kevin yelped. He fumbled back into the bedroom, muttering under his breath.

"What happened?" I asked, "Who was it? What's going on?"

"Oh, it was that lady who comes here and buys eggs every week," he said breathlessly.

"What did she want?" I asked. She certainly wouldn't be at the door in the middle of the night to buy eggs."

"The goat," Kevin gasped. "She was coming down the road and suddenly there was that white goat out there and she thought he was loose."

"Oh," I moaned. "So that was it."

Kevin sat up angrily. "She shone a flashlight right into our kitchen!"

Suppressing the urge to giggle, I suddenly realized what the problem was. Kevin didn't have a stitch of clothing on! I figured it must've scared his egg customer as much as it did him.

7

PIG PROBLEMS AND POLKA DOTS

Shortly after we got the pig, Kevin decided it needed to be castrated. This was one area I definitely was not going to get involved in. My association with the pig ended in the kitchen where his food was dutifully stuffed into the large, white container.

However, I did make a comment about the local veterinarian, upon which remark Kevin replied indignantly, "Vet? Why should I pay a vet when so-and-so up the road, who has pigs, knows how to do it himself?"

To argue would have been pointless, but by now I had learned Kevin's so-called short cuts, in the long run, always cost us more money. I told myself wisdom dictated I should keep my mouth shut and let Kevin learn the hard way. Of course, in the end, I did open my mouth with the oft repeated, "I told you so." And furthermore, Kevin did *not* learn anything!

I cannot recall the particular day when the pig expert came to meet with Kevin and our unfortunate pig, so I must've driven into town to shop. Heaven knows, I was up to my eyeballs with things to do, and therefore had plenty of reasons to be absent.

We had committed to a weekly Bible study in our home and on top of that I volunteered to put together a prayer chain. After securing an out-dated church directory, I began the tedious and complicated task of matching up people for this telephone ministry. After two or three weeks of concentrated work, I proudly presented the completed list to the church.

Several days later I received a phone call from one of the women on the list. "Thank you for putting together the prayer chain," she began, and then continued with the word I had most dreaded to hear, "***but***…it won't exactly work."

"Oh?" I asked with disappointment. "Why not?"

"Well," she drawled, "you see, many of the people who are supposed to be involved are deceased."

Just to make sure I had heard her right, I asked, "Dead?"

"Yes," she stated apologetically. "Dead."

I hesitated as my mind ran two laps around the track. Couldn't it be remedied? "Well," I finally replied, "if you would like to inform me who is still alive and who can be involved on the prayer chain, then I'll redo it."

She agreed and in the days to follow I managed to edit the lengthy prayer chain and bring it up to snuff. I just hoped nobody else associated with that church died for a long time.

Meanwhile, back at the ranch, something was happening to that pig. He wasn't doing well, and finally, after days of surveillance, Kevin conceded that the pig was in trouble, big trouble.

"This time," I said with authority, "we've got to call the vet."

Grudgingly he agreed and made an appointment for the vet to come out to our place. I must've had my head stuck in a bucket, or was elsewhere when he made that phone call because the next thing I knew he was giving me instructions about the vet's untimely visit.

"Okay honey," he ordered as he headed out the door one morning at six o'clock, "I'm going to the church to the men's prayer meeting to pray for our pig and you get dressed and be ready for the vet."

Shocked, I looked at him in horror and disbelief. Why me? But before I could answer, the door slammed and he was getting into his car.

No sooner had I slipped into a pair of jeans and a sweatshirt than the vet was banging on the door. All the kids were fast asleep, or pretending to be. I grudgingly followed the vet to the odoriferous pigpen and fearfully followed him to the side of the suffering animal.

"Where's your husband?" asked the vet, after sensing that he was not dealing with country-bred woman.

"He's at church, praying for the pig," I replied soberly.

He squinted at me with an expression that was hard to fathom. Finally, he turned to the work at hand. "Oooo-kay," he said firmly, "I want you to hold his head down. You'll have to put your knee on his head and hold him steady, no matter how much he screams and wiggles."

I knew without a doubt that this incident was not going to be one of my most fond memories. Anger began to rise as I thought of Kevin, all nice and clean, sitting piously in that prayer meeting while I was wrestling in the mud with a stinking pig. My idea of farm life, (once upon a city time), was harvesting wonderful fresh vegetables, canning, entering the fair, walking in pastures green, watching blazing sunsets over the distant hills, riding well groomed horses along happy trails, and living happily ever after.

Ever since Kevin and I had married and moved to the country, it seemed that most things had been a hassle. As the anger mounted, it lent strength to my puny 105 pounds, and boy, did I ever need it! The vet, without anesthetic, cut into that poor pig. I can't believe to this day that its ear-piercing screams weren't heard fifty miles away. All I knew was I had to keep his head and shoulders still, but everything within me wanted to plug my ears and run as fast a I could out of that horrible pen.

Finally, it was over and the vet motioned for me to let the pig up. I was trembling uncontrollably. "Ma'am," he said with a shake of his head, "tell your husband that the next time he wants to castrate a hog to call me. You see," he explained, "there's folks around here who think they know how to do the job, but they botch it up and this is what happens." He showed me a big ball of skin and pus and God-knows-what he had cut off that pig.

I stumbled back to the house and ran into Craig. "Hi," he said lamely.

"Didn't you hear that pig screaming?" My voice had risen to near hysteria.

"No," he mumbled sleepily.

"You mean to tell me," I was panting by now, "that you didn't hear anything?"

"Well no. What do you mean?" He ran his fingers through his tousled hair.

"Oh never mind!" I retorted and marched into the bedroom. When was I ever going to get wise over this animal and vet set up?

Some time later, when the pig was well recovered, I decided I needed a day off. It was sunny and hot and just right for getting a tan. Nobody happened to be home and so I put on my little yellow polka dot bikini and plopped out on the sun deck. Ah, such peace and privacy. At last, time to relax, reflect and . . .

Suddenly, I heard a noise in the garden. Peering over the edge of the deck, I spotted that priceless Hampshire porker snorting through the garden. I had no time to lose, and quickly jumped into my tennis shoes. Tearing down the steps and out into the yard I noticed a short two-by-four leaning against the fence. Grabbing it up I tore after that pig.

Now, if you can, picture this: A yellow polka dot bikini clad woman, long twin ponytails flying, wildly chasing with a board in hand after a panicked pig! Around and around the yard we went.

About that time two of our neighbors, who were men from the church, happened to drive by in their car. I'll never forget the astonished looks on their faces as they slowed to a crawl to watch what must've been an unforgettable scene.

Finally, the pig dashed around the chicken pen and into his own mucky space. I quickly slammed the gate shut and walk briskly back to the house.

By the time I showered and dressed, it was getting late. The quiet, private moment on the deck had been completely shattered, and I could just imagine the conversation going out through the prayer chain about Mrs. Liebenthal chasing a pig around the yard with a two-by-four, dressed in what?

It was time to call Peggy, and confide in her my latest embarrassing adventure. It seemed I was calling her more frequently as the days went by. When she finished snickering, she said, "You really should write a book."

That was a phrase I heard more and more often as time went by.

8

FOOD AND FIRE

When I was a kid one of the many rules at the dinner table was that I was to eat everything on my plate whether I liked it or not. Thank God my mother was a great cook, and I liked most of the stuff she made. Granted, not all of it was tuned to my taste buds, however, but I couldn't leave the table if I didn't clear my plate. My parents meant what they said, so I managed to chew and swallow certain things or I'd still be sitting there.

Therefore, I fully intended to carry over my parents' rules about never wasting food because there were poor children in China starving to death. Of course I never could figure out how my choking down mashed parsnips or egg plant, which I hated, could help some poor kid in China! I figured they wouldn't like it either, even if they were starving.

One night I made a huge pot of spaghetti with spaghetti sauce. For some reason which I'll never know, the kids weren't enthused with it so there were plenty—like a LOT—of leftovers which I reheated and dished onto their plates the next night. And the next night, and the following night...I think this went on for almost a week! It was the food standoff of the decade. They wouldn't eat it, and I wouldn't cook anything new until they did. My husband finally spoke up and put an end to the impasse by suggesting we feed it to the farm animals, and that I should make something else.

Okay, well, here's the thing. I cooked (and still do) with whatever the grocery store happens to have on sale. One day I brought home a beautiful beef heart which I prepared the way my mother taught me, all tender, well-seasoned, and nestled in sage dressing. I have to say, I was quite proud of the way it turned out and, while not expecting a round of applause, figured everyone would be overjoyed.

To say I was deluded about that is an understatement. While my husband smacked his lips in appreciation, the kids were all in a flap, making faces while audibly expressing their horror and displeasure at eating organ meat with sounds that I can't spell.

So, off the table and into the fridge it went. After a couple of days I hatched a plan that involved "cooking camouflage". I carefully cut the meat into pieces that resembled sliced roast beef, warmed it, made nice mashed potatoes and I can't remember what else but they gulped it down, raving about how it was so tender and "the best roast they had ever eaten." To this day they have no clue as to what they enjoyed so much that night!

Thus, I not only became an expert at sorting food and garbage for the outdoor members of this "farm family", but I also became an expert at recycling and repurposing leftovers and "unwanted" food for the "indoor members" as well!

Then there was the day of the kitchen fire. If there is anything I am terrified of it is fire. I think one reason I never took up smoking cigarettes when other teens did is because I was scared to death of striking matches, or even lighters. Besides, I thought that smoking was dirty, stinky, unhealthy and a total waste of money. So, when my big kettle I was heating oil in to make popcorn for a new popcorn cake recipe caught on fire because I was preoccupied with a phone call I about panicked. Bright yellow flames were shooting up out of that pot, blackening the stove vent and surrounding area. Somehow my brain kicked in and I grabbed the lid which I threw on top of the flames. I have to admit, I was both shaken and shocked—shaken because a little oil could combust into a mini inferno so quickly, and shocked that the fire was actually out and that the whole place hadn't burned to the ground.

Thankfully, nobody was home to see my stupid blunder, but boy oh boy did I ever have my work cut out for me! My nice, clean white kitchen had a big sooty streak around the stove and white cupboards that was going to tell on me. Somehow, like the "white tornado" I got the whole thing cleaned up and in order before anybody came home!

9

GHOST RIDERS IN THE SKY

One afternoon, Kevin announced that he was going to go to the livestock auction and look for a calf before driving to work. I knew better than to ask what we needed a calf for, but silently wondered how our small pasture could possibly support a calf along with two horses.

I busied myself in the kitchen and waited for his return. *It will be interesting,* I thought to myself, *how he is going to get a calf in that small station wagon.* I was comforted by the thought that at least this latest addition to the Liebenthal farm was not in any way my responsibility, problem, or duty. No sir, this time the entire beef-raising endeavor would be out of my hands. I would simply refuse to get involved.

I heard the car roar into the driveway and jerk to a stop. I peered out the window to see if the baby had arrived, but saw nothing except for Kevin panting his way up the steps. "I got a great deal on a range calf," he motioned to me as he burst through the door.

"Where is it?" I asked. He shot me a look of exasperation.

"He's coming. I mean, well, after I bought it several cowboys and myself couldn't get it into the station wagon."

I felt my eyes widen. Just how big was this wonderful range calf anyway?

Kevin went on. "It just didn't look all that big from my bench way up in the auction barn. I was just positive I could get it in the car.

Mental images of this recent rodeo at the auction yard ran through my mind. It must've been quite a scene. I supposed those cowpokes would laugh about that one for some time to come. I knew better, however, and managed to keep a straight face.

"Now," Kevin ordered, as he prepared to shower and change, "they're bringing the calf some time tonight. You don't have to worry about it because I told them exactly where to put him."

Relief nearly had a chance to sweep over my soul when Kevin added the proverbial "but". "But," he ordered, "please go out tonight and make sure that the calf isn't scared so he'll want to stay in the pasture. And, take him some grain in the bucket."

"Uh huh," I responded unenthusiastically. It was probably going to be just my luck that the thing wouldn't be delivered until way past dark, and my bedtime.

"Now, remember," Kevin reiterated. "This is a calf that's been on the range. That means," he leveled his gaze on me, "that he's rather wild, you know, not used to people."

After Kevin went to work, it seemed I waited around forever. The kids were all asleep and I was exhausted. Finally, I decided to get ready for bed. Perhaps the cowboys weren't going to deliver that calf after all. And, I reasoned, if they did happen to bring him, I could just slip on my bathrobe and go out to the gate and check on him.

No sooner had I changed into my nightgown than I heard the cattle truck pull into the driveway. I couldn't tell exactly what was going on, as it was pitch dark outside. Finally, after much scuffling, mooing, and banging, the truck pulled out of our place. I listened as the roar of its engine faded into the night.

This should be easy, I told myself. All I had to do was take some grain out to the gate, talk nicely to the calf, and then retire for the night. I went downstairs, dipped the pail in the grain and walked out into the night.

It took my eyes a few moments to adjust to the darkness and when they did, I spotted the shadowy form of a half-grown cow in the pasture. With lowered head, he cautiously faced me.

"Nice boy," I crooned as I gently shook the pail of grain. "It's okay." *Oh brother,* I thought to myself. *How could Kevin have not seen that this thing is huge!*

He snorted and backed up a step. "Aw, come on." I said, trying to sound reassuring. "Come get some nice grain."

Suddenly, he let out a bellow, turned and charged to the far end of the pasture that bordered the Black's place. I could hear him crashing through the brush, or was that the fence? "Oh great, "I muttered to myself. "Now I did it. Panicked Kevin's cow." As I began to think about how that nervous Hereford saw things, I suddenly realized my pale pink, shimmering bathrobe must've looked like a spook to him. *Oh no!* I though with horror, *He thought he saw a ghost and took off! Kevin's gonna kill me because I have the distinct feeling that critter is no longer in our pasture.*

I fell into bed and pondered the situation. There was no way I could run around in the dark, chasing that cow. Besides, if I did find him, I couldn't persuade him to get back into our pasture. *Well, that beef sure thought he saw "ghost riders in the sky."* In spite of myself, I giggled.

Early the next morning I jumped out of bed as soon as the geese sounded the alarm that Kevin was home. I knew the first thing he would do would be to scan the pasture for his newly acquired prize. I listened to his approaching footsteps as he ascended the stairs. "Hi. Didn't they deliver the calf?"

"Uh, yes," I answered and quickly added, "and I did just exactly what you told me to do so he wouldn't be scared, but he's really a wild thing and ran off in the dark." I could see he was thinking about my explanation. "Why?" I ventured. "Isn't he in the pasture?"

"No."

"Oh."

Kevin yawned. "Well, I'm not surprised, I guess. Cows don't like to stay in a pasture all by themselves, so he's taken off to find others of his own kind.

I was relieved Kevin wasn't going to explode in my face. But he wasn't finished, no, not by a long shot.

"I've worked all night, and I'm really tired. So, I'm going to bed and perhaps Peggy can go with you today to find that cow."

And that was that. I got dressed and called Peggy. She was always up early, taking care of her pigs. After explaining the situation to her, she chuckled and agreed to go with me through the surrounding countryside in search of the missing cow. *I always wanted to be a cowgirl,* I thought, *but I'll just have to ride my imaginary horse on this one.*

We went from farm to farm, asking if they had sighted a lone Hereford. Most of them had seen him, but none of them knew where he went. This continued day after day for an entire week.

Finally, we approached a hog farm several miles from our place. Yes, they had seen him, and yes, he had gone through the fences out in back of their place, and yes, we could go through their farm in search of him.

Crawling through barbed wire was never one of my talents and it seemed it took forever to cover a small space. In spite of Peggy's assistance, I ripped the seat of my jeans. But, we couldn't turn back now since the trail was getting "hot".

Peggy was well in front of me when I climbed over a board fence to take the most direct route to the woods in the back of the hog farm. Half way through the enclosure, I suddenly realized a large gathering of pigs were closing in on me. I began to run, remembering one of my dad's favorite sayings, "I haven't had this much fun since the pigs ate my little brother." (I believed him for years, and still wonder if it really happened!)

The faster I ran, the faster those grunting, beady-eyed, hungry porkers ran. Finally, I reached the fence. Believe me; I got over it as good as any stunt man in Hollywood could have.

Peggy was waiting for me on the other side. I didn't dare explain to her my panic. After all, she was an expert with hogs. All I knew was, those ham hocks didn't get this chicken for breakfast!

She gave me a knowing grin, however, and then led the way through the pasture and out to the forest. We didn't find the cow that day, either. But, all I cared about was finding another way back to the main road so I could get home, shower, and put on another pair of jeans that had a full seat in them.

The next day the phone rang and Kevin answered it. "Good news! I know where our calf is," he announced.

"Where?" I was ecstatic. No more life-threatening adventures through people's pig pens.

After explaining that the calf was contentedly living with another of his own kind miles from our place, he and the kids jumped in the station wagon to pay him a visit. I still couldn't figure out how Kevin was going to get that jittery range cow back to our place and then keep him in the pasture. If there was anything I had learned in the past week it was this: once a cow gets its head through a fence, the whole cow is through that fence!

Well, this story has a happy ending. Kevin made a deal with the woman whose pasture the calf adopted, that she would allow it to stay there until it was ready to butcher, and then she would get half the meat.

I was extremely relieved and so was Peggy!

10

I'M RIGHT, SOMETIMES

"We need to put a radio in the hen house," Kevin announced one morning.

"What for?" I asked, "So they can listen to the news?"

Kevin didn't think it was funny. In fact, nothing I every said or did was funny to him. Everybody else thought my adventures were hilarious. Peggy and Ted were beginning to have serious second thoughts about the "normalcy" of our family and told me quite often that I should write a book.

"Chickens lay better if they have music," he said matter-of-factly. "I read it."

"Okay," I replied. "That's fine with me."

Later that day Kevin came up with a battered old radio. The kids and I followed him out to the hen house and watched as he placed it high in the corner opposite the nesting area. Plugging it in, he turned the dial until he picked up a rock n' roll station.

"Don't play that junk," I protested. "They won't like it."

I received icy stares from four pairs of eyes, but I held my ground. "How do you expect these poor chickens to want to lay eggs if their nerves are all screwed up?"

More icy stares. Finally, Kevin said, "They will like it, you'll see. We'll get more eggs than ever before."

"Okay, it you say so," I resigned and stomped out of the chicken house.

The next day I decided to take a neighbor up on her offer to horseback ride on her land. I figured it was my turn to go horseback riding. If one of the kids went with me, then surely I'd get farther than a city block. Theresa said she'd be happy to go and so we prepared for the ride.

I prided myself in being able to curry and saddle my own horse. I made sure the cinch was tight, being privy to the horse's ability to puff up like a balloon so the cinch would loosen later. Everything was going well, and sure enough, both horses dutifully made the pilgrimage up the shady road to our friend's drive. Once she saddled up, the three of us rode out to the back of their property where there were miles of trails.

We followed her as she and her horse picked their way down a hill to a bubbling creek. *This just has to be heaven, I told myself. All I ever do is work. What a great day this is. I should do it more often.*

Of course, nobody knew I was terrified of falling off of a horse and getting hurt. My motto when it came to horses was, *stay on no matter what.* I lived up to that motto, too, even when on a trip in previous years to Montana where I rode my cousin's palomino. He took off on a dead run, and, to my way of thinking, was faster than Man-O-War. At full speed ahead, the clever horse flew under a low tree branch, but since that failed to unseat me, he charged up to a fence where he slammed to a stop. True to my motto, I stayed with him, but believe me, I was shaking like a leaf in the wind.

After riding around for a while, our guide led us up a steep hill. Half way up I noticed there was more distance between my mount's ears and me than when we had first begun. The cinch! It was so loose the saddle was slipping back to the trail end of the horse. *If that saddle goes off the back, I reasoned, I go with it!* There was only one thing to do, and that was hang on to her mane with all my might.

Theresa saw the problem and encouraged me in my efforts to keep the saddle and myself upright until we crested the hill. Somehow it worked and I was able to dismount and tighten the cinch. I never did figure out how that horse managed to hold so much air!

For the next few days Kevin grew increasingly moody as his egg production drastically fell off. Then one day he came in the house with a puzzled expression on his face. "What's the matter?" I asked.

"Well," he said hesitantly, "the chickens somehow flew up and knocked the radio down and they broke it."

"Oh, really?" I smiled and then, I just couldn't help myself. I added, "I guess they didn't like that awful rock n' roll garbage."

After that, the egg production soared. That was one time I was right.

The girls had a pet hamster that they kept upstairs in their room. The problem was, the little rodent kept getting out of its living quarters. Then the hunt would be on to find him. I began to lose my patience over their sloppiness, (in more ways than one) in keeping their pet corralled. "Look," I told them one day, "if you don't secure the lid to this co-called cage, then this glorified mouse is going to get loose and we'll never find it."

I can truthfully say the one thing that was consistent with those girls was disregarding any advice on my part.

Not long afterward, I began to notice a horrible, ghastly smell in my bedroom. It soon became apparent something had died in the wall, right next to the head of the bed. Needless to say, I became suspicious and cornered Connie and Theresa. "Is that hamster in its cage?" I asked.

They looked at one another, wide-eyed. "Well?" I persisted.

"Um," Theresa began, eyes downcast, "it sort of disappeared about three days ago."

"Oh great!" I exclaimed. "Do you want to know where it is?"

"Yeah! Where is he?" chimed Connie and Theresa in unison.

"Dead in my bedroom wall!" I was thoroughly disgusted and they knew it.

"Oh no," Theresa said sadly.

"We couldn't help it," Connie said defiantly. "He just wouldn't stay in his cage and when we weren't looking, he got away."

"You should've listened to me in the first place," I said. "Now our bedroom stinks to high heaven.

"It was no use. Any sympathy that may have been in their hearts was for their unfortunate pet, not for me.

One day Kevin decided he needed to divide the pasture so the horses wouldn't overgraze the whole thing at once. His plan was to run a single wire from the house, across the pasture to the other side of the creek.

"Are you positive this wire is going to keep that horse on one end of the pasture?" I asked him.

"Of course. It's going to be electric. Horses won't go through electric fences."

"But," I argued, "that horse is good at escaping. I really can't see how this itsy bitsy wire is going to. . ."

His look silenced me. Oh well, if this is what he wanted to do then more power to him. The project seemed to take a long time, and all the while he worked on it the mare stood at the end of the property and watched him.

Now, mind you, that mare was intelligent, which wasn't a good thing where Kevin was concerned. On top of that, she definitely had a mind of her own. Nearly once every week or so, in the middle of the night, she would do a Houdini act, and escape the confines of the pasture, galloping full speed ahead, with our gelding following her, down to a church member's ranch where a prized Arabian stud lived. Then, invariably, the phone would ring, waking everyone up, with the news that our horses were out, *again.*

Kevin would get the girls up so they could join him in chasing down those horses. He knew I was useless for the job, because it usually took me at least an hour, and a cup of tea or two, after rising from bed to be fully awake. Besides, those horses ran, snorting and kicking, (and letting out great bursts of gassy air), when they were being pursued. He knew I was afraid of getting my head kicked off. Thus, I got to stay in bed.

As it turned out, the man and the horse were in a contest to see who had the final say about the pasture and the fence. When the job was done and the electricity was flowing, Kevin proudly stepped back to survey his magnificent achievement. "Okay," he said with confidence, "let's just see her get through this!"

I turned and looked at the mare. I could see her wheels turning. Then, as if reading our minds, she backed up a few steps, lowered her head and charged at a full gallop down the creek. To our amazement, she flew right under that wire, ripping it loose.

"How on earth did she do that?" I yelled. "She was running through water, and right under an electric wire!"

Kevin's tightened jaw was twitching. Turning on his heel, he stomped into the house and got ready for work. That horse had won another round and, unfortunately, once again, I was right.

11

TO CHASE AND BE CHASED

By this time I began calling our place the "Liebenthal funny farm." The pesky goat had managed to not only eat most of the blackberry leaves around the perimeter of the property, but he had devoured all my flowers as well.

One day, when I was alone, the goat got loose and headed for the vegetable garden. In a panic, I dialed our pastor. After all, "minister" means "servant" and right then I desperately needed help.

His oldest teenage daughter answered the phone. I asked for her father and told her I needed immediate help to round up our goat. I heard her sarcastic voice on the other end of the line as she said, "It's Mrs. Liebenthal, *again*. She wants you to go help her catch her goat.

Soon our good-natured pastor arrived and together we managed to wrestle that goat through the gate to the pasture. Not being as clever as the horse, I figured that goat would stay busy in the pasture until Kevin returned.

As time went on, Kevin began to search longer and harder for places to tie the goat. One day he tied the goat's chain to a low tree branch.

In the meantime, we had acquired another dog. He was a beautiful sable shepherd who simply showed up. His favorite resting-place was on top of my car where he would dangle his front paws over the windshield as if admiring his shapely legs. He adopted me, and I was delighted to have somebody in my corner.

On the day the goat was secured to the tree limb, I went for a walk in the pasture with my new four-legged friend. Suddenly, I heard a loud crack as the goat successfully broke off the tree limb. Much to my horror, that goat lowed his head and charged me. I took off running, as fast as I could, across the field with the goat close behind, dragging the tree limb and my new dog on the heels of the goat. What a scene it must've been!

Once I reached the fence, I quickly ducked under it. Then I saw a pair of dress shoes and nice trousers. Looking up from my gritty place in the dirt, I saw my dad laughing his head off. He had driven all the way from the city to visit. His only regret was that he hadn't brought his movie camera!

Kevin couldn't be content with the zoo at hand and met someone who was giving away a couple of geese. You guessed it; he brought them home, in boxes, in the back of that sorry station wagon.

Much to my surprise, these geese were brown. I was of the impression there were two kinds of geese—white ones and wild Canadian ones.

Now, these new arrivals began to take charge of the pasture and the chicken pen. They were sassy, ornery, and just plain mean, especially the male. I could no longer go out to the hen house to gather eggs, for that male goose adopted the area right in front of the gate for his very own territory. Puffing out his feathers, he shook, rattled, and hissed, defying even the most determined egg gatherer to get past him.

Mrs. Brown Goose eyed him with disapproval as if to say he was getting carried away. Therefore, I stayed on my side of the fence, weeding and tending the garden.

Kevin also managed to get some ducks from some place or the other, and I obligingly tossed slugs to them from the garden. It was rather sickening watching them gobble down such disgusting creatures. But at least the ducks didn't chase me around the place.

One day the tax assessor came to the door. She was pleasant, but I wasn't happy to see anyone representing the oppressive tax system. She asked a few questions, and then decided to walk around the outside of the house. I watched her from the windows. Soon all the geese were squawking, flapping, and running, necks outstretched, toward the terrified woman. Mr. Brown Goose led the pack, hissing and rattling his formidable feathers. The last thing I saw of the tax assessor was her car hastily backing out of the driveway.

One day I spotted two of the neighbor's pink pigs roaming around our yard. Yelling for Kevin, (the kids weren't home), we raced out into the yard. *Heaven help them,* I thought, *if they get in my garden!*

"They're Jason's pigs from across the street!" Kevin yelled. "We've got to get them back over there."

"Okay," I agreed and dashed into the carport. Spotting a cheap, plastic yellow rope, I quickly looped it into a lasso. Now was my chance to prove what a great cowgirl I would've made.

We ran those elusive pigs around the yard a few times, and then I saw my chance. Tossing the loop at just the right moment, I watched with delight as it settled over the pig's head. Pulling it tight, I halted my imaginary quarter horse and smiled triumphantly.

My victory was short-lived, however, because that dumb excuse of a rope didn't hold the knot and my catch got away! I always did remind folks, however, that I really did lasso a pig.

Between Kevin and me, we finally got Jason's pigs chased back into their pen. While we were in their yard, I spotted what

Jason and his family considered to be a vegetable garden. I shook my head in disgust. Weeds and vines were inches higher than the vegetables and the entire plot was overgrown with grass.

Later that evening I took a quick drive down to the dairy farm. On my way home, I decided to pull into Jason's place to let them know their pigs had been out. Even though we spoke to one another, we had never been inside of their home. The outside looked dumpy and run down, and when they invited me in, I was hesitant, not knowing what to expect.

As I stepped into the living room, my eyes widened in surprise. The interior of their home was beautifully decorated, orderly and clean. Jason, noticing the shock registered on my face, offered an explanation.

"Surprised?" he chortled, "well, it's like this. We figure as long as the outside is unkempt and full of weeds and junk, then our taxes will stay low. Them tax people have no idea how this place looks on the inside."

I had to agree with him. No one would've guessed how tasteful and pleasant the interior of their home was. He explained how they didn't have to weed their garden because the weeds gave the slugs something to eat other than the vegetables. Still dazed, I bid them farewell and began to walk home.

"Excuse me," Jason's wife called after me, "but aren't you forgetting something?"

"Oh," I replied. "What's that?"

She motioned toward the driveway. "Your car."

12

THE DAY THAT THE RAINS CAME

Fall came in all its beauty and splendor. The garden had been harvested and jars of canned beets, carrots, pickles, string beans, as well as fruit filled the pantry.

The Hampshire was nicely wrapped and in the freezer. There was much to be thankful for.

Kevin and the kids were shopping in town, and I was left to enjoy the blissful peace and quiet. The sky was dark and heavy with clouds. I knew it was going to soon unload buckets of water, so I quickly filled several containers with water from the sink.

One of the first problems we discovered when we moved into the house was the water system. The water mains were antique and made of wood. Whenever it rained for any length of time, mud and silt came right through the tap, along with God-knows-what-else. Our hot water heater and toilet tank were full of mud. Usually the lines broke, and we went without water for up to several days at a time.

Satisfied that we had plenty of water, I busied myself in the kitchen.

Meanwhile, rain began pounding in earnest. I watched the water bounce on the paved road and collect in pools. No doubt about it, it was going to be quite a storm.

Soon the little creek that I had originally thought of as harmless began to roar in earnest. I walked into the bedroom where I could get a better look at it. Part of the pasture near the pond was under water. The horses stood on higher ground under the eaves of the house.

Darkness began to descend and still Kevin and the kids weren't home. I checked the pasture again and this time saw that the creek had overflowed its banks and the chicken pen was flooding.

The telephone rang and I dashed to pick up the receiver.

"Hi, this is Peggy. How are you doing down there?"

"Oh, Peggy," I cried, "I think we're flooding and Kevin isn't home yet."

"I'm going to send Ted down there," she said. "There must be something in the culvert if you're flooding."

"Thanks, Peggy. I just can't imagine what could be caught in that culvert."

After dark, Kevin arrived home. I was mad, and he knew it.

"What's the problem?" he asked cheerfully.

"Thanks to you, the culvert was plugged and our pasture flooded, including the chicken yard."

"What do you mean?" he asked.

"Ted had to come down and risk his life to unplug it because you had put that old wood lawn furniture upstream, in the trees. Whatever did you do that for?"

He looked at me as if I had two heads. "So I could sit up there if I wanted to."

"Well," I retorted, "did you ever sit up there?"

"No," he replied.

"Those chairs floated downstream and got caught in the culvert," I explained. "Everything backed up. It was awful."

"Well," he responded, "nothing drowned did it?"

"How should I know?" I shot back. "Do you think I was going to wade around out there to find out? The ducks and the geese and the horses were all right. I just assumed the chickens would go up their ramp and into their house."

As it turned out, the door had been shut at the top of the ramp, and a couple of poor chickens had met their fate in the flood. Otherwise, everything came out all right except the goldfish that had been in the front yard suddenly appeared in the pasture swimming in the duck pond.

After that, Kevin made sure nothing was placed around that creek which could wash downstream into the culvert.

One of my regrets was every time the pastor came to call I was either busy mopping the kitchen floor or shoveling ashes out of the Franklin stove. It happened so frequently, that I began to suspect he had some sort of tuning device that told him I was cleaning so he could come calling.

One Sunday his sermon was entitled, "Will You Be Remembered for Your Mop Bucket?" I was positive that the entire message was directed at me. At the conclusion I knew what I would be remembered for if I didn't change my ways. I could just see the epitaph on my tombstone: Here lies Mrs. Liebenthal, who had the cleanest floor in the world.

After that Sunday, I never mopped the floor until late at night when I knew there was no chance that anyone would be coming to call!

13

THE CITY GIRL IN THE COUNTRY

There was no way to salvage our reputation with Peggy and Ted. Without a doubt, they regretted ever proclaiming we were a normal family!

I have often wondered, *just what is normal?* My conclusion is Adam and Eve were "normal" before they blew it in that infamous Garden of Eden. Therefore, none of us are "normal!"

One day I decided to visit a very poor family in our area. In the back of my mind was the desire to invite them to Sunday school and church, or at least be able to witness to them. As I pulled my car into their cluttered front yard, barefoot kids, dirty from head to toe, ran out to greet me. Excitedly, they led me into their small, cramped house that they shared with an assortment of dogs and cats. "Look at our kittens!" Twinkling eyes and a shy smile radiated out of a little girl's dirty face. "Can you *please* take a kitten? We *have* to find homes for our kittens."

I should've known that no amount of resistance on my part was going to make one iota of difference to the persistent children. How do you explain to little kids such things as being allergic to cats? Before I knew it, sympathy for a fluffy, pure white, blue-eyed kitten won out and I was on my way home with one sad, sorry kitten loaded with fleas.

Now, by some miracle, up to this point, we didn't have fleas in our house. All that changed, though, when I dunked the poor creature into a nice warm sudsy bath in my bathroom sink. Fleas began to crawl, hop and jump every which way. Not having previous experience with flea infestations, I didn't pay a whole lot of attention to that problem. My focus was on that sweet little kitten. I knew he wouldn't survive for long in our "zoo" as we lived on the corner of two busy country roads. Therefore, I got him a good home with an animal loving friend.

So, the kitten left, the fleas stayed, and they loved me in particular. One day I had to dress up and go to the city to run an errand at the courthouse. As I walked down the sidewalk, suddenly I could feel one of those blasted fleas crawling around on my stomach, under my underwear. I wanted to rip everything off right then and there and nail that thing, but tearing off one's clothing next to the police department (or any other public place, for that matter) is simply *never* acceptable! A nice looking gentleman who walked up the sidewalk towards me and then passed by will never know how desperately a woman he passed that day wanted to scream, squiggle, scratch and squish a flea under her clothing!

By this time I figured I owed myself a break. Since I loved to sketch and paint, I decided to grab my sketchpad and find a nice spot to draw. Rummaging through Kevin's old camping gear in the basement, I located a folding canvas stool. *Ideal,* I told myself. I figured in order to ensure nobody would bother me I needed to hike across the road and set the stool up facing Rachel's place. From this vantage point I could see the creek gurgling its way beneath lush green branches as it wound its way through her pasture.

I had barely begun the sketch when suddenly, without warning the campstool canvas gave way ripping right through the middle, and I found myself sprawled in the gravel alongside the road. Slowly I collected my bruised parts and stooped to pick up the scattered drawing pencils. Tucking the treasonous stool under one arm and my sketchpad under the other, I marched home with as much dignity as I could muster.

Through the church fellowship, we met a new family to the community. I instantly felt a kinship with Polly who, with her husband Bill and small daughter, had left the city life for country life.

As soon as they were settled in, we paid them a neighborly call. It didn't take long for me to discern Polly didn't know a thing about the country. Suddenly, I was an expert.

"Did you know that roosters don't lay eggs?"

"Really?" Polly said. "How come?"

I was on a roll. I informed her of the many different kinds of chickens, pigs, cows, and geese. She was fascinated and wanted to hear all about our farm life.

Kevin, on the other hand, wanted to be helpful. Helpful, that is, to us as well as to Polly and Bill. He told them about how wonderful goats are to clear the land of blackberry bushes and weeds. After making a good sales pitch, he volunteered to loan them our goat, free. Such a deal!

A couple of weeks after the goat had been relocated to Polly and Bill's place, we paid them a call.

"By the way," Polly said, "that goat gets under the house and we can't get him out."

"Really?" I answered.

"On top of that," she continued, "he likes to climb up on top of the car."

"Oh dear," I mumbled.

"Is he doing a good job on the blackberry bushes?" Kevin asked.

"Yes, but he's a lot of trouble," Polly said.

You've got that one right, I thought to myself.

"The other day," she gestured wildly, "I was out in the yard and bent over to pull a weed when, all of a sudden, wham! That stupid goat butted me in the rear end and slammed my head into the house."

By now I didn't know whether to laugh or cry. But, Polly was good-natured about the whole thing, and soon she was asking more advice. "What do you know about raising a pig?" Polly asked.

"Well," I began, "let me tell you. . ."

These poor city folks, I thought. *They have a whole lot of things to learn!*

And so ends the true story of THE PIG AND I.

www.ingramcontent.com/pod-product-compliance
Lightning Source LLC
Chambersburg PA
CBHW071103040426
42443CB00013B/3382